THE OXFORD GUIDEBOOK

by
Alan Crosby, D.Phil.

CONTENTS

© Alan Crosby, 1989

(First published as Seeing Oxford, 1982; revised 1984, 1986, 1987)

Oxford Books is a series published by Trans Atlantic Investments Limited
Blair House, Church Lane, Somerton, Oxford OX5 4NB

ISBN 1 871144 05 1

OXFORD'S PAST

Oxford is a beautiful and magnificent city, famed throughout the world for its splendid buildings, its lovely streets and open spaces, and its fascinating past. That past is the key to an understanding of the present, for everywhere in the city bears the imprint of history, and as you walk through the streets you will constantly be reminded of centuries of colourful events and illustrious people.

It is said that the city was founded by King Alfred in the 9th century. Although this is subject to dispute, there is no doubt that Oxford began as a Saxon town. The site of the city was a long narrow belt of drier land between the marshy valleys of the Thames and Cherwell, the two rivers which are still so important to the life of Oxford. At the centre of the Saxon town, near the top of a low hill, was a crossroads. 1,200 years later this place is as important as it ever was. It is called Carfax, which means "four ways", and there the four main streets — High Street, Queen Street, Cornmarket Street and St. Aldate's — meet.

Oxford became a market centre for a large area around, and soon developed as the administrative capital of that district, which was called Oxfordshire. In 1002 the city was burned by the Danish invaders, but quickly recovered, and when the Normans conquered England in the 1060s they made it into a leading military centre. A strong and powerful castle was built in the 1070s by Oxford's first Norman sheriff, Robert d'Oili, on the western edge of Oxford; most of it has now disappeared. The impressive St. George's Tower survives today, and is among the finest of the buildings in the city, remarkably well preserved for its age. Unfortunately it is not open to the public, because it is in the grounds of Oxford Prison, but you can see the great "motte" or mound of the castle from New Road, on the way to the railway station.

The young city also became known as a place of learning, when scholars and theologians began to move there as religious houses were founded. By the 1190s there were students and teachers, and in the 1250s Oxford University was formally established. It was soon recognized as one of the foremost intellectual centres of Europe: Oxford University is the oldest in Britain. The religious communities were also celebrated, and in the mid-14th century there were no fewer than eight large abbeys and priories within a radius of four miles of Carfax.

During the 12th century the city acquired the close links with royalty that it has retained ever since. In the Civil War of 1135–50, between King Stephen and the Empress Matilda, the latter was imprisoned in the castle. Legend has it that she escaped by being let down from a high window in a basket, and then fled across the frozen marshes dressed in white for camouflage. Her son, King Henry II, is said to have visited his mistress, "Fair Rosamond", at the nunnery of nearby Godstow, the ruins of which may still be seen. King Richard I, "the Lionheart", was born at Beaumont Palace in Oxford in 1157: the palace has now vanished, but its name is perpetuated in Beaumont Street, which lies across its site.

As the university grew, during the Middle Ages, many houses were demolished to make way for colleges and halls, so that by the 16th century these occupied about a quarter of the old walled city. The inhabitants who were displaced moved outside the walls, and new suburbs grew up along the roads leading into the city. St. Giles was one of these: its unusual width is due to its being the place where cattle and sheep were herded, before they were driven into the city itself for sale at the market. Oxford prospered, and over the centuries acquired its superb heritage of fine colleges, halls, churches and houses, with the whole city crowned by a skyline of towers and spires.

During the Civil War of 1642–9, London was held by the anti-Royalist Parliamentary forces; King Charles I made Oxford his capital, and lived here for several years. He resided in Christ Church while his Queen, Henrietta Maria, was lodged at Merton College. The city was refortified during the war and although most of the works have now disappeared they are recalled by the names North Parade and South Parade for two streets in North Oxford, these being the places where the troops were paraded.

During the 18th century there was another period of building by the university and colleges, and some of the best of the buildings of Oxford date from this period: Worcester College, Queen's College and the Radcliffe Camera. The city was fortunately bypassed by the Industrial Revolution, and thus was spared the manufacturing development which spoiled so many English towns in the late 18th and 19th centuries. Although there were a few industries, including printing, brewing and marmalade-making, Oxford remained a town dominated by the university.

Until 1870 university lecturers were not allowed to marry, but when this rule was ended many did so, and built large houses for their new families in North Oxford. This area, along the Banbury and Woodstock Roads, is today famous for its immense Victorian houses, set in wooded gardens along tree-lined streets. In 1912 William Morris, a former bicycle maker (and no relation to the poet and artist of the same name), began to build cars at Cowley, a village just beyond the south-east edge of the city. After the First World War Morris, later Lord Nuffield, expanded the new industry, and during the 1920s Oxford was transformed from a sleepy old-fashioned market town into a bustling manufacturing centre, famous not just for a university but also for cars, such as the Morris Oxford. The city sprawled as its population grew rapidly, from 67,000 in 1921 to 96,000 in 1939 (today it is about 110,000).

Since the Second World War Oxford has continued to flourish as a centre for modern industries, as a commercial and shopping magnet, as a great focus for educational, scientific and cultural activities and, of course, as an attraction for visitors from all over the world. There have been many changes during this century as progress has made its mark. Some new roads, many new shops, urban renewal and the expansion of the university have altered the appearance of parts of the historic city but, in essence, the heart remains surprisingly intact, and is a source of delight to residents and visitors alike.

Cupola of Queen's College by night

THE UNIVERSITY AND THE COLLEGES

Visitors to Oxford often ask, quite understandably, "Where is the University?" The simple answer to this is, "Nowhere and everywhere". Oxford does not have a campus-style university such as is found almost everywhere else in Britain and in other countries. Instead the University of Oxford is widely spread through the city, so that there is no building or group of buildings which can be pointed to as "The University".

The University of Oxford is the body which examines for and awards degrees, and which shares in administration. It has a historic church (St. Mary's on High Street), a vast and world-famous library (the Bodleian), numerous departmental libraries, several museums of international repute, a publishing house which is one of the finest in the world (Oxford University Press), an extensive and beautiful park in North Oxford, and many administrative buildings. The university, as is the case elsewhere, has a large number of departments and schools, each of which comes under the control of a *Faculty Board,* and through these bodies it appoints and employs a proportion of the total staff. The university authorities are responsible for the external relations of the whole system, for example, conducting negotiations with the Government. The university is headed by the *Chancellor*, who serves either for life or until resignation, and has honorary and ceremonial duties. The *Vice-Chancellor* is the "prime minister" of the university, and is elected from among the heads of colleges to serve a four-year term. Administrative power is held by the *Hebdomadal Council*, the "cabinet", composed of senior members of the university and colleges, and by *Convocation*, the graduates of the university with M.A. status who form the "parliament" but have little real power. It is the responsibility of the *Senior* and *Junior Proctors*, the "magistrates" of the university, to see that administration is carried out efficiently, and that discipline is maintained among the students, who number almost 12,000.

There are 35 colleges within the university, and a number of *permanent private halls*, which are attached and whose students are allowed to read for degrees, but which remain outside the control of the university. Colleges are independent entities, which own their own buildings and facilities, and administer them quite separately from the university. They are therefore different from the Halls of Residence found in other universities. Each has a *governing body*, made up of senior members of the college, and this appoints the head (in Oxford usually called a *principal, master, warden* or *provost*).

Colleges select and admit the undergraduates, most of whom will have taken the special Oxford Entrance Examination set by the university. All candidates are interviewed by one or more colleges of their choice before being accepted or rejected. The students are members of their college as well as of the university. Most live and eat in college, and there they can participate in social, sporting and cultural activities, but there are also innumerable societies and clubs organized on a university basis. Among these are the university sports teams, including the famous "Eight" which competes annually in the Boat Race against the rival University of Cambridge.

It is perhaps easiest to visualize the relationship between the university and the colleges as a federation which benefits both sides. American visitors may find it helpful to think of the colleges as being equivalent to the individual states and the university to the Federal Government. A link is provided by the teaching staff, who are always members of a college, and at the same time are engaged in teaching for the university. Many are *fellows* of the colleges (that is, senior members) but are also lecturers, readers or professors of the university. They are popularly known as *dons*, a word which derives from the Latin *dominus*, meaning "master".

A don directs the studies of those undergraduates of the college who are reading his or her subject, setting and marking essays and meeting with them, usually in pairs, once a week for an hour in a tutorial, to discuss their work. Dons also give lectures at their department building to an audience drawn from the colleges of the university and they form *faculty* or *departmental committees*.

Tradition is a vital part of the life of Oxford University. Its very organization dates back to its origins in the 13th and 14th centuries, and if it now seems confusing to you, do not worry — many students spend three or four years here and still find it all very difficult to understand!

Encaenia procession in Broad Street

SOME OXFORD TRADITIONS

Although many of the traditions of Oxford University date back almost 800 years, it is inevitable that there have been some changes more recently. Many of the names and titles which are used are the direct descendants of words of medieval Latin, and the academic dress which is worn more often in Oxford than in any other university is also very similar in many respects to medieval student dress. Undergraduates today do not have to wear the medieval-style gowns for normal university works but academic dress is still compulsory for all formal and ceremonial occasions. Less frequently worn is the mortar board, the square tasselled cap of the male students and lecturers, or the small square cap which is worn by women. The full dress is obligatory for all examinations and degree ceremonies, and is called subfusc. During May and June, when examinations are in progress, the streets are frequently crowded with students in traditional black and white subfusc, making their way to or from the Examination Schools at the lower end of High Street.

On several Saturdays each year you may see a more splendid sight outside the Sheldonian Theatre in Broad Street, when degree ceremonies are being held. Then the area is crowded with students and dons wearing their full academic robes, including gowns with colourful hoods. The degree ceremonies take place in the Sheldonian Theatre, and are conducted entirely in Latin, another survival of the medieval origins of the university.

The most impressive of all these ceremonies is the Encaenia Procession, when all the highest officers and dignitaries of the university, including the Chancellor, wear their most elaborate and beautiful robes, in pink, gold, crimson, grey and scarlet, most of them similar to those worn six centuries ago, and process through the streets of the city to the Sheldonian Theatre. The ceremony inside involves the awarding of honorary degrees of the university to illustrious figures from other universities, from the arts, politics and sciences, and to distinguished people from other countries. At the ceremony, which is also entirely in Latin, public speeches or orations are made.

Other university occasions are much less formal, and many are purely social. The inter-collegiate rowing races are held on the Thames, off Christ Church Meadow, in February (these races are known as Torpids) and in late May (known as Eights Week). Then the banks of the river are lined with crowds of spectators, cheering their colleges and enjoying one of the great social events of the Oxford calendar. On May Morning, the first day of May, a choir sings carols from the top of Magdalen Tower at dawn, around 6 am. The road is closed, and Magdalen Bridge is crowded with early risers. Later in the morning there are celebrations in High Street, Broad Street and Radcliffe Square, with morris dancing, music and stalls, and many people breakfasting in the open air.

In June many colleges hold all-night Balls, and there are performances of plays in college gardens.

Degree ceremony in the Sheldonian Theatre

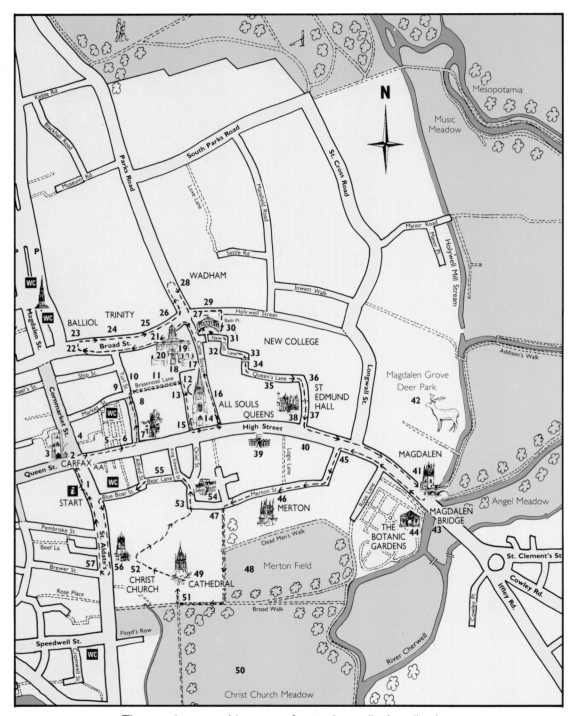

The numbers on this map refer to the walk described.

A Guided Walk

Our guided walk will take you to all the sights in the ancient and beautiful centre of this historic city.

We follow a circular route, starting and finishing at the Oxford Information Centre, but of course it can be joined or left at any point. To follow the route, you can use the accompanying map: the numbers on this refer to those in brackets in the description of the walk. More detailed information on the different colleges will be found in the section "Colleges Described" which follows this guided tour.

Begin at the Information Centre in St. Aldate's. Facing the busy street, which runs gently downhill from the heart of the city, you will see opposite the late 19th-century Town Hall (**1**). Inside, is a large and richly decorated main hall, where concerts are often held. Beneath the building are the cellars of the medieval Guildhall, now skilfully converted into the Museum of Oxford (entrance in Blue Boar Street, to the right of the Town Hall; admission free).

From the Information Centre turn left, up the hill, and walk towards Carfax (**2**) at the top. This crossroads is the busiest place in Oxford, as the volume of traffic — both wheeled and on foot! — will testify, and has been the focal point of the city for more than 1,200 years. The name derives from a Latin word meaning "four ways". Here stood one of the most ancient churches in the city, St. Martin's; it was pulled down in 1896, but its medieval tower, now known as Carfax Tower (**3**), was left standing. See the brightly painted figures, half-way up the front of the tower, strike the bell when the clock chimes. Those with a head for heights can climb the tower and obtain an unusual view of the city centre, the Castle Mound and the surrounding hills.

From Carfax start to walk eastwards to the High Street. Looking to your left, along Cornmarket Street, you can just see in the distance the Saxon tower of the city church of St. Michael at the Northgate. Cornmarket Street is one of the principal shopping streets of Oxford, and has been so for centuries; the name is derived from the medieval corn market which was held here. On the right you will see a pair of very large grey wooden gates at the entrance of the Golden Cross Shopping Arcade (**4**) — which leads into the Covered Market — reconstructed from the courtyard of the 16th- and 17th-century Golden Cross Inn. Shakespearean plays were reputed to have been held here. The arcade is extremely attractive with several small specialist shops.

Continue down High Street, which has been described as one of the finest streets in the world. It curves away from Carfax down a gentle slope, and is lined for most of its length with magnificent buildings which together make a superb streetscape. On a busy day, crowded with traffic and people, High Street's charms may be harder to see, but in the early evening or on a Sunday morning this remains one of the great sights of the world.

On the left is the delightful Victorian Covered Market (**5**), originally built in 1774. It is reached by four passageways or "avenues" between the shops of High Street. Enter the market along one of these passages, and wander round. A fascinating mixture of sights, scents and colour awaits to greet you: tempting cakes and pastries, freshly baked breads and pies, bunches of scented flowers and herbs, shiny fruits and vegetables, hand-made chocolates, pastas, salamis, braces

of grouse and pheasant, gleaming salmon and trout, the delicious aroma of coffee and exotic teas.

On your return to High Street continue left, past the Mitre Inn (**6**), once owned by the Bishops of Lincoln and in the 18th century the most celebrated of Oxford's many coaching inns. Opposite are several 17th-century town houses, now largely converted into shops but still keeping their distinctive gabled upper storeys. Just past the Mitre, on the other corner of Turl Street, is the early 18th-century church of All Saints, now Lincoln College Library (**7**), and beyond that the lovely curve of High Street.

Turn left into Turl Street, also known as "The Turl"; this narrow road derives its name from the "twirl", a turnstile gate in the old city wall at the far (Broad Street) end of the street. There are three colleges in the Turl: Lincoln (**8**), Jesus (**9**) and Exeter (**10**). The view down the street includes the huge chestnut tree which overhangs the wall of Jesus College on the left. Opposite the entrance to Market Street turn right, into Brasenose Lane. This quiet back lane is the last street in Oxford with a central gutter, a channel running down the middle instead of gutters along the edge which are now found everywhere else. A central gutter for drainage was a characteristic feature of streets throughout medieval Europe. To the left are the walls of Exeter College, to the right those of Lincoln College and Brasenose College. The large trees which overhang the lane on the left, and which in summer add so much to its shady peace, are in the beautiful Fellows' Garden of Exeter College (**11**).

Ahead of you can be seen the walls of All Souls College (**16**). At the far end of the lane you will emerge into Radcliffe Square, the heart of the university area and with unquestionably one of the finest groups of splendid buildings to be seen anywhere in the world: the Radcliffe Camera, the University Church of St. Mary the Virgin, All Souls College and Brasenose College,

and the Old Bodleian Library.

The Square achieved its present form in the 18th century although most of the surrounding buildings are older than that. The centre-piece is the Radcliffe Camera (**12**), built in 1736–49 with money bequeathed to the University of Oxford by Dr. John Radcliffe, an eminent physician; it cost £60,000, a vast sum for those days. The building is circular in plan and has false columns around the outside; the large dome, at the time of its construction the largest in the country, is a most distinctive feature of Oxford's celebrated skyline. The Camera is now a reading room for the Bodleian Library, and so is not open to the public. The square which it occupies was, in medieval times, an area of closely packed streets and houses: these were gradually demolished as the university and colleges undertook new building and planning schemes over the centuries. Today only the line of the two streets or lanes at either edge of Radcliffe Square serves to remind us of its ancient origin.

Turn right towards High Street again, walking along the edge of the Square past Brasenose College (**13**). Ahead is the great church of St. Mary the Virgin (**14**) the largest in the city and the official church of the university. It occupies all of the southern edge of Radcliffe Square, and its tall spire soars above the other buildings of the city as well as its immediate surroundings in a most impressive and dramatic way. Before visiting the church continue down the narrow lane, once known as School Street; notice the houses on the right and, in particular, the elaborately carved and painted wooden canopy over one of the doorways (**15**). Turn left into High Street, and here pause to look once more at the beauty of this street, with All Souls College (**16**) beyond the church, and lower down the columns and dome of the façade of The Queen's College (**38**). Between the two colleges is another of the great overhanging trees which are so prominent in the streetscapes of central

High Street view of University Church of St. Mary the Virgin, Radcliffe Camera and Queen's College to the right

All Souls College

Earl of Pembroke, Bodleian Library

Oxford and which provide such a fine setting for the golden-yellow college buildings.

As you walk past the church, notice the giant twisted "barley sugar" columns of the 17th-century south porch. Then turn left into Catte Street, now a quiet pedestrian lane but until the early 1970s a busy road choked with traffic. Pay a visit to the church: the interior, with its huge windows and splendid monuments, is very impressive. If you feel adventurous, climb the tower to the base of the spire, and enjoy the best of all panoramic views of the city and surrounding countryside from above. On leaving the church continue around the Square, walking to the right of the Radcliffe Camera. On your right is All Souls College (**16**), with its large and richly ornamented wrought iron gateways and a multitude of pinnacles and turrets. Further along is the huge west window of the college's Codrington Library. At the end of the Square, ahead to your left, go through the arched doorway into the Schools Quadrangle of the famous Bodleian Library (**17**), pausing to look back at the Radcliffe Camera.

The Bodleian Library, the main library of the University of Oxford, is one of the largest, richest and oldest in the world. In 1610 the Library secured the right to a copy of every book published in this country, and so became the first copyright library; there are now five others in the British Isles. The Bodleian has over four million books, countless papers and pamphlets, priceless manuscripts and many works of art.

The Schools Quadrangle, which you are entering, is so called because the different schools of the university each had a separate section here: their names are still beautifully painted over the wooden doors around the quadrangle. The building dates from 1610–24, and is notable for the simplicity and symmetry of its design, at once light and graceful yet imposing. Above the main entrance, to your right, is the Tower of the Five Orders, which is so named because its design incorporates each of the Five Orders, or styles of classical architecture. The statue in the quadrangle is that of the Earl of Pembroke, Chancellor of the University, 1617–30.

Enter the glass doors behind the statue, and visit the Divinity School (**18**), across the entrance hall. The Divinity School was built in 1420–90 and is memorable for its exceptionally fine lierne vaulting, a particularly delicate form of fan vaulting, completed in 1483. The building is one of the triumphs of English medieval architecture, a wonderful setting for the exhibitions held here.

Return to the Schools Quadrangle, back through the glass doors, and leave by the entrance to your left. You will emerge on to the gravelled courtyard in front of the Clarendon Building (**19**), named after Edward Hyde, Earl of Clarendon (chief minister of Charles II, 1660–73, and father-in-law of James II). The Clarendon Building was designed by the celebrated architect Nicholas Hawksmoor, and built in 1711–15 to house the Clarendon Press, later renamed the Oxford University Press. The Press eventually outgrew its premises and in 1830 moved to an extensive site in Walton Street. The Clarendon Building is noted for its great triangular pediment and portico on the Broad Street side, and the superb wrought iron gates, a feature typical of Hawksmoor's work.

Look to your right, across Catte Street, for a good view of the Bridge of Sighs (**32**), built in 1913–14 by Hertford College to link their two buildings on either side of New College Lane; the bridge is loosely modelled on the famous bridge of the same name in Venice. Now cross the gravelled courtyard to the Sheldonian Theatre (**20**) built in 1664–9. This is not a theatre in the modern sense of the word, but instead was, and still is, intended as the setting for the ceremonies held by the university, including the granting of degrees. It was the earliest major classical

Cupola of the Sheldonian Theatre

Emperor's Head, Broad Street

17

building in the city, and was also one of the first (and best) works of Christopher Wren, the architect of St. Paul's Cathedral in London, and Professor of Astronomy at Oxford. The main entrance is at what appears to be the rear of the building, facing the Divinity School. Ceremonial processions and dignitaries enter here through the enormous double doors. Inside, the seats are arranged in semi-circular tiers beneath a ceiling painted by Robert Streater. Concerts are regularly held here, and you may climb up to the lovely cupola for another splendid view of the spires and pinnacles of Oxford.

Descend the steps into Broad Street, noticing the Emperors' Heads (**21**). They are among the finest and certainly most familiar of Oxford's many carvings and statues, and were part of Wren's original design. They are not, in fact, the heads of emperors, but are free interpretations of classical figures from Rome and Greece. Their precise identity and origin remain something of a mystery. In the 1970s they were renewed after serious decay.

Turn to your left at the foot of the steps and walk along Broad Street, passing the Old Ashmolean Museum, the oldest museum building in Europe, and now serving as the Museum of the History of Science. At the corner of Turl Street look at the view to your left, with the tower and spire of All Saints filling the gap between college buildings. Then continue along Broad Street past *The Oxford Story*, where you can experience a fascinating and enthralling audio-visual history of the University of Oxford, spanning the last eight centuries. Where the separate carriageways rejoin, opposite Balliol College, look in the middle of the road for a stone cross (**22**) set in the surface. This marks the place where, in 1555, the Protestant Bishops Latimer and Ridley and, in 1556, Archbishop Cranmer — three of the leading figures of the English Reformation — were burned at the stake, under Catholic Queen Mary I. The Oxford Martyrs, as they were soon called, are

Blackwell's Bookshop

New College gate

commemorated by the Victorian Martyrs Memorial just north of St. Mary Magdalen Church in St. Giles.

Broad Street was formerly the site of the town ditch, called Cam Ditch, which ran along the outside of the city walls. Cross the road to Balliol College (23), with its 19th-century façade, and then walk back towards the Sheldonian Theatre end of the street. You pass the gates of Trinity

The curve of the High Street

College (24) and the attractive 17th-century cottages, typical of those which once lined many of the streets in the city centre. From this part of the street there is a good view of the Sheldonian Theatre and the imposing portico of the Clarendon Building with its great pillars. On the other side of the street can be seen Sir George Gilbert Scott's superb slender spire of Exeter College chapel rising above the rooftops.

Beyond the cottages you come to Blackwell's Bookshop (25), famed throughout the world. It is housed in an interesting 18th-century building, once a town house. The New Bodleian Library (26) is immediately adjacent to Blackwell's. It was built in 1937–40 after the older library had become hopelessly crowded and full. The "New Bod", as it is commonly known, is typical of the architecture of 1930s Oxford. Glimpse the charming elephant on the weathervane of the History Faculty building (27), the former Indian Institute, at the crossroads ahead.

At the traffic lights turn left and walk a short distance down Parks Road to look at the elegant façade of Wadham College (28), set back from the road behind a smooth green lawn. The Kings Arms, on the corner of Parks Road and Holywell Street, is an old Oxford pub which is a favourite haunt of undergraduates. Return to the traffic lights and turn left into Holywell Street, and walk along it as far as the Holywell Music Room (29). This plain but delightful building dates from 1742–8, and was the ancestor of modern concert halls, being the first building in Europe specifically designed and built for musical performances. Two and a half centuries later it is still fulfilling its original purpose. Holywell Street has more surviving 17th- and 18th-century houses than any other street in central Oxford, and in recent years most have been restored and re-painted. A good view of the houses, with their attractive variety of sizes, architectural details and colourful paintwork can be obtained from this point, the whole street making a very pleasant picture.

Almost opposite the Music Room is the entrance to Bath Place (30), perhaps the most quaint and tucked away part of the city centre. It is the last survivor of the cobbled yards or courts, which were once a characteristic feature of Oxford. Its houses, which date from the 16th and 17th centuries, lean at odd angles and have pastel coloured paintwork. The medieval town ditch, which we have noted in Broad Street, passed through the site of

The Bridge of Sighs, Hertford College;
tower and chapel of New College beyond

*Magdalen College and Botanic Gardens
on the River Cherwell*

now characterizes the university and colleges. St. Helen's Passage runs between high dark walls to emerge on to New College Lane almost beneath the Bridge of Sighs (**32**). The bridge frames a fine view westwards to the Sheldonian Theatre, Clarendon Building and Bodleian Library.

Turn left along New College Lane, and around the double bend in the lane visit New College (**33**), one of the largest and most splendid of Oxford's thirty-five colleges. Then return to the lane and continue left under the second bridge. New College Lane is typical of the back streets of "old" Oxford and, despite yellow no-parking lines and the tarred road surface, it retains to this day something of its medieval atmosphere. Notice as you proceed by the old-fashioned lamp-standards, the towers and pinnacles of All Souls College (**16**) over the high wall to your right and on turning left, the superb series of carved heads and gargoyles high along the buildings of New College (**34**). Ahead on the right is the great library building of Queen's College (**35**), a very fine piece of early 18th-century classical architecture, crowned by a caryatid, a winged statue. Along the lane, at the next bend, the church of St. Peter-in-the-East (**36**) comes into view. This dates from the 11th and 12th centuries, and is now the library of St. Edmund Hall. The library is not open to the public but visitors may enter its impressive and cavernous crypt, one of the finest in the city.

St. Edmund ("Teddy") Hall (**37**) itself is on the left just past the entrance gates to the churchyard, Access to the library is through the delightful and intimate Front Quadrangle of the college. It is a very great contrast to the magnificence of New College, and the two neighbouring colleges perfectly illustrate the way in which Oxford combines architectural splendour with quiet beauty. On reaching High Street turn right, and visit (The) Queen's College (**38**), noting the long and sweeping curve of High Street looking up the gentle slope

Bath Place, and is still marked by a depression in the ground, which is why the courtyard slopes down from the street: the houses are actually built across the site of the ditch. Go down Bath Place and at the end turn left, through the very narrow, low arched passageway, into the garden of the Turf Tavern (**31**). The Turf is the oldest and by far the most picturesque of the many public houses and taverns in the city of Oxford. It lies at the foot of the great city wall — this is one of the best surviving stretches of the medieval defences — and close to the bell-tower of New College; the chiming of bells is well known to customers of the tavern. The narrow pathway continues through the yard of the Turf Tavern and then turns to the right, to become St. Helen's Passage. Notice here how the new buildings of Hertford College have been cleverly fitted into the cramped and confined space, a good example of the care for architecture and history which towards the city centre. The view from the corner of Queen's Lane and High Street includes the dome and façade of Queen's College itself, the spires of St. Mary the Virgin and All Saints, and All Souls College. On the other side of High Street is the long frontage of University College (**39**). Retrace your steps passing the entrance to Queen's Lane, where the Coffee House on the corner is built on the site of the oldest coffee-house in Europe, dating from the 1630s. On the other side of the road is the stately and imposing Examination Schools building (**40**), built in the same Jacobean style as the Town Hall. It was constructed in 1877–83 and is used for all university examinations. In May and June the street outside is crowded with students entering or leaving their examinations, accompanied by numerous friends offering good wishes, moral support or commiserations!

Continue along High Street, past the row of shops which occupies 17th-

Mercury Fountain, Christ Church

century town houses, the upper floors being student accommodation for St. Edmund Hall. Keeping to the left, cross Longwall Street. As its name implies, this street ran alongside the city wall, but the long high wall which can be seen on the right-hand side of Longwall Street is the 15th-century boundary wall of Magdalen College (**41**). The city wall ran behind the houses on the left-hand side of the road.

Ahead, along High Street, can be seen the tall and lovely tower of Magdalen College, rising high above the street, and the long pale golden front of the college. The tower is often considered to be the most beautiful in the city, and its setting enhances a fine piece of architecture. Every May Morning (May 1st) a choir sings from the tower at 6.00, a ceremony which dates back to medieval times, and which is one of the highlights of the Oxford calendar. Try to spend some time in Magdalen (pronounced Maudlin) College, with its cloisters, riverside walks and deer park (**42**). On leaving, turn left along High Street and go as far as Magdalen Bridge (**43**), the eastern approach to the city for two thousand years or more. The present bridge, over the River Cherwell, was built in the late 18th century. It offers a good view of the river which, in the summer, is crowded with rowing boats and that characteristic craft of Oxford's waterways, the punt.

Cross the road in front of Magdalen College to the other side of High Street, where you may visit the 17th-century Botanic Gardens (**44**). Turning towards Carfax, walk down to the Eastgate Hotel (**45**). As its name implies, the hotel was built on the site of the ancient east gate of the old walled city. Here turn left into Merton Street. Opposite the hotel entrance, you will see the beautiful wrought iron gates and splendid clock of the Examination Schools.

Merton Street is a quiet, cobbled back street, with an attractive mixture of domestic and college architecture. Until the 1970s, the old lamp-standards in this street and New College Lane were still lit by gas. On the right, around the first bend, is the rear of University College and the Examination Schools, and, on the left behind the high wall, the gardens of Merton College. Merton College (**46**) is one of the competitors for the title of "oldest in Oxford", and the charming Mob Quad of the 1350s is unquestionably the earliest surviving quadrangle in the university. Just past Merton College chapel, turn left down a narrow gated pathway — Merton Grove — overhung by trees. Corpus Christi College (**47**), with its attractive pelican sundial, is on the right.

At the end of the path go through the iron gate and continue straight ahead for a few more yards. To your left is the open space called Merton Field (**48**). If you look back across the field you can see one of the best-preserved stretches of the medieval city wall, with the 17th-century buildings of part of Merton College behind. There is also a particularly attractive view of Magdalen College tower rising over the trees and rooftops. If you then look through the arched gateway on the right-hand side of the path you will see some of the private gardens of Christ Church and beyond them a very good view of the tower and spire of Oxford Cathedral (**49**), which is also the College Chapel.

Continue ahead until you reach the wide gravelled road known as the Broad Walk. This divides Merton Field from the larger and more rural Christ Church Meadow (**50**) which is ahead of you. The Meadow is a marvellous survival, a piece of grazing land only yards from the centre of a busy city. It has never been ploughed and has never had chemical pesticides and fertilizers used on it, so it is unusually rich in wildlife and has many rare plants and insects.

If you wish to go down to the Thames to see the river and its boating and rowing, there is a circular walk along tree-lined banks around Christ Church Meadow. Otherwise, turn to the right along Broad Walk, towards the large and prominent

Meadow Buildings (**51**) of Christ Church, clad with Virginia creeper, built in the 1860s. Pass through the entrance gate into the college (small fee payable).

Christ Church (**52**) is the largest, richest and most magnificent in the university. Within its precincts are the Cathedral, the Chapter House and the Picture Gallery, which houses some of the extensive collection of art treasures owned by the college. The route through the buildings and quadrangles is well-signposted for visitors to enable you to see all the major features, and exits on to Oriel Square (**53**). As you pass through the college, by way of the splendid Cathedral, notice the vast Tom Quad (this is the great Front Quadrangle of the college, named after Tom Tower, the bell-tower over the entrance which houses The Great Tom bell; "Old Tom" chimes 101 times every evening as it has done for over 400 years), the statue of Mercury in the middle of the water-lily pond full of huge carp, and the sundial on the wall as you leave the quadrangle to the north.

To leave Christ Church, turn left into Oriel Square (**53**), passing by Oriel College (**54**) to reach King Edward Street, which is distinctly Edwardian in character.

Turn left into Bear Lane, named after the Bear public house visible in front of you at the corner of Alfred Street. Notice the recently restored Quartermaines Stables on the right (**55**). On reaching the Bear turn left into Blue Boar Street; on the left are 1960s buildings of Christ Church, neatly tucked into the limited space available. The street passes beside the Museum of Oxford to emerge on to bustling St. Aldate's.

Here turn left for a short distance to look at the magnificent façade of Christ Church, built in the 1520s and surmounted by the majestic dome of Tom Tower (**56**), another of Oxford's favourite landmarks. Then cross the street and pass by the ancient St. Aldate's Church (**57**), to return to the City Information Centre from where you started your walk.

Christ Church Meadow

Eights Week

COLLEGES DESCRIBED

To many people the university and its colleges *are* Oxford, and nowhere in the city centre is far from a building of beauty and interest belonging to one or the other. With its libraries, colleges, departmental buildings and halls, the University of Oxford has an architectural and historical heritage almost without rival in Britain.

Omitted from the entries below are colleges not in the historic centre of Oxford. Most colleges are open during the afternoon, from 2 pm until 5 pm during the summer. Others are open during the hours of daylight.

★ **All Souls** *(1438: King Henry VI and Archbishop Chichele of Canterbury)* High Street and Radcliffe Square — This college could be described as Britain's most magnificent war memorial: it was founded in memory of those who died during the Hundred Years War between England and France. Its splendid buildings of beautiful golden-yellow stone stand in a prominent place next to the historic church of St. Mary the Virgin, and form a major feature of the architectural grandeur of Radcliffe Square and High Street. The Front Quadrangle dates from the 1440s and the North Quadrangle, behind, from 1722–30. The latter is famous for its beautiful wrought iron gates leading on to Radcliffe Square, and for the twin telescopic towers designed by Nicholas Hawksmoor. Other important features are the 15th-century chapel and the Codrington Library begun in 1716. The college has the distinction of being open only to Fellows: it takes neither undergraduate nor postgraduate students, and its members are instead elected to Fellowships after distinguishing themselves by their later research, or as an academic honour. They include many famous names from politics, economics and the social sciences, and election to a Fellowship of All Souls is deemed to be one of the highest honours in the academic world.

★ **Balliol** *(about 1250: John de Balliol)* Broad Street — Most of the buildings are of the 18th and 19th centuries, although the college is one of the four oldest in the university, and claims to be the oldest of all. The Broad Street frontage is of 1867–68, and is by Waterhouse, the designer of Manchester Town Hall. Between the Outer and Inner Quadrangles are wooden doors which were scorched by the flames which burned to death Archbishop Cranmer and Bishops Latimer and Ridley, when they were executed in Broad Street in the 1550s for their Protestant beliefs.

★ **Brasenose** *(1509: William Smyth, Bishop of Lincoln)* Radcliffe Square — The unusual name is taken from the "Brazen Nose", a great brass door-knocker which originally came from the Hall (a semi-academic residential building for students of the university) which stood on this site in the Middle Ages. The proper name of the college, which is scarcely ever used, is "The King's Hall and College of Brasenose". The Old Quadrangle, entered from Radcliffe Square, dates from 1509–14, with a third storey added in the early 17th century. It is one of the best-preserved buildings of its date in Oxford. The chapel (1656–66) has a superb vaulted roof of fan tracery, and the New Quadrangle (1880s) is an excellent example of the Arts and Crafts architecture of late 19th-century Oxford.

Tom Tower and Mercury Fountain, Christ Church

★ **Christ Church** *(1525: founded as Cardinal College by Thomas Cardinal Wolsey)* St. Aldate's — This is unquestionably the most splendid of the colleges, as well as the largest, and is often known simply as "The House". Visitors must enter through the Memorial Gardens lower down St. Aldate's. The great Tom Tower, above the main entrance, is by Sir Christopher Wren (1681) and houses "Great Tom", a huge medieval bell which once belonged to Osney Abbey. Behind it is Tom Quad, the largest quadrangle in Oxford, with the famous fountain and statue of Mercury in the centre. The quadrangle, built by Wolsey, was intended to have a cloister all round but he fell from power and it was never completed. The stone plinths which would have supported the columns of the cloister still can be seen. The buildings of the college were in part those of the ancient abbey of St. Frideswide, and the church of the abbey became the chapel of the college. In 1545 it was also made the cathedral of the new diocese of Oxford (see page 49). Take a look at the superb vaulted hall, the largest of any Oxford college, and the 18th-century Canterbury and Peckwater Quadrangles. Those interested in art should also visit the Christ Church Picture Gallery (in the Dean's Garden), where some of the large and valuable collections of the college are on display (see page 47).

★ **Corpus Christi** *(1517: Bishop Fox of Winchester)* Merton Street — Among the smallest of the colleges, it is tucked away down a quiet side street, and is often passed by. The Front Quadrangle dates from the 1520s, and was enlarged in 1626. In its centre is the famous Pelican sundial, first erected in 1581. The chapel is early 16th century, and the tiny Fellows' Quadrangle, the smallest in Oxford, was built in 1706–12.

★ **Exeter** *(1314: as Exeter Hall by Bishop Stapleden of Exeter)* Turl Street and Broad Street — The original buildings have all disappeared, and the quadrangle dates from the 17th and 18th centuries, restored and altered in the mid-19th. The best part of the college is probably the chapel, built in 1854–60 to a design by Sir George Gilbert Scott, based on the Sainte Chapelle in Paris. The tall, slender spire is a prominent central Oxford landmark, seen to advantage above the rooftops from neighbouring Ship Street.

★ **Hertford** *(1740, then closed in 1818 and refounded by T.C. Baring, M.P., in 1874; constituent halls date back as far as 1282)* Catte Street and New College Lane — The main buildings date from 1818–22 and were extended in 1887. They face the Bodleian Library, and are an important part of the classic view towards Radcliffe Square and the University Church of St. Mary the Virgin. In the late 19th century the college bought a second site, on the opposite side of New College Lane, and to link the two halves it built the celebrated Bridge of Sighs in 1913–14. Although a comparatively new feature by Oxford standards, the Bridge has become one of the best loved and most photographed Oxford landmarks.

★ **Jesus** *(1571: Dr. Hugh Price, with the patronage of Queen Elizabeth I)* Turl Street — Part of the First Quadrangle is 16th century, and the whole of the Second Quadrangle dates from the early 17th. The chapel, of 1621, is one of the best surviving examples of Jacobean religious architecture, while the Hall, in the passage between the two quadrangles, is an excellent illustration of the old-fashioned style of Oxford college halls, with its moulded and painted ceiling,

Keble College, part of the façade with its Victorian decorative brick-work and the chapel beyond

wooden panelling and many paintings. Jesus College has, since its foundation, been closely associated with Wales, and many Welsh students still go there.

★ **Keble** *(1870: by subscriptions raised by the Anglo-Catholic Oxford Movement)* Parks Road and Blackhall Road — This was the first of the new colleges, Hertford (1740) being the last of the older ones. Keble is the only college founded by public subscriptions, under the auspices of the Church of England, the money being raised to educate men of academic ability but of limited means. It was built in memory of John Keble, Fellow of Oriel College, Professor of Poetry and a leading religious revivalist of his time. The remarkable design, by William Butterfield, is an outstanding example of the Victorian Gothic style. The buildings are of red brick with stone banding and chequered patterns, a wonderfully lively contrast to other college buildings. The excellent chapel, with its soaring heights and glowing mosaics, contains Holman Hunt's famous Pre-Raphaelite painting, "The Light of the World".

★ **Lincoln** *(1427: Richard Fleming, Bishop of Lincoln)* Turl Street — Although Lincoln College is in the heart of the city it is comparatively little known. The most notable architectural feature is the almost unchanged Front Quadrangle and Hall, completed in 1437, and still with the original bell rung for chapel each evening. The Hall has a timbered louvre, a vented opening in the roof to allow smoke to escape: this is an extremely rare example of such a device, and it is the last in Oxford. The chapel (1629–31) has scarcely altered since the day it was completed. The library, on High Street, is housed in the outstanding early 18th-century church of All Saints, one of the most distinctive features of the Oxford skyline, with its beautiful golden-white tower, cupola and spire rising above High Street.

★ **Magdalen** *(1458: William de Waynflete, Bishop of Winchester)* High Street — Magdalen (pronounced *Maudlin*) is second only to Christ Church in size and splendour, and in the scale and quality of its architecture. The most impressive feature is the magnificent tower, built in 1492–1509, one of Oxford's finest landmarks. It soars 144 feet sheer from the pavement of High Street, and is crowned with tall pinnacles forming a splendid crown, the whole being prominent in many views of the city and High Street. From the tower a choir sings at 6 am every May Morning, in a charming traditional ceremony. The chapel (1474–80) is noted for the quality of its music: to hear a choir singing here is to experience something of the atmosphere of the Middle Ages. The cloister is, with that of New College, the best example in Oxford, and remains complete, giving an impression of the cloister of a medieval religious house. It has a large and ancient wisteria, which in the early summer fills the air with its heady scent. Through the narrow passage at the far end of the cloister is the wide lawn fronting the classical New Buildings of the late 1730s, and beyond them to the left is the college's own deer park, which has been in existence since the foundation and which still provides venison on special occasions. To the right of the New Buildings is a pair of wrought iron gates, through which one can reach the delightful tree-shaded walks along the River Cherwell.

Magdalen College tower

★ **Merton** *(1264: Walter de Merton, Chancellor of England)* Merton Street — The college is one of several competitors for the title of "oldest in Oxford", is the oldest with an unbroken history as a collegiate foundation, has the oldest buildings in the whole of the university, and has the oldest surviving medieval library (1337–8). The example of collegiate planning (staircases leading off a square or rectangular quadrangle) set by Merton was followed by almost every Oxford college right up to the present day. The charming Mob Quad of the 1350s is the earliest surviving quadrangle in Oxford. The chapel was begun in the 1290s intended to be a parish church, but was never completed; the impressive tower, elaborate in design, with pinnacles and turrets, was built in 1448–51.

★ **New College** *(1379: William de Wykeham, Bishop of Winchester)* New College Lane — From the name it is clear that newness in Oxford is relative, since the college is rather more than six centuries old! The original name was "the St. Mary College of Winchester in Oxford", but as there was already a St. Mary College (later Oriel) in Oxford, it became known as New College instead. The Front Quadrangle, with its golden buildings, oval of smooth green lawn and, in early summer, beautiful magnolia tree, is a superb example of 14th-century design; it was extensively altered in the late 17th century. The ante-chapel and chapel are noted for the extensive collection of medieval stained glass; the huge and towering 19th-century screen, and the controversial 1951 statue "Lazarus" by Epstein. The cloister, beyond the chapel, is dominated by the tall detached bell tower, and beyond the Front Quad, wrought iron gates erected in the 18th century give access to beautifully laid out gardens, which are bounded in part by one of the best-preserved stretches of the medieval city wall, complete with bastions and ramparts. The large mound in the centre of the garden is a medieval landscaping feature, adapted in the Civil War as a Royalist gun emplacement. The buildings along Queen's Lane have an excellent series of grotesque gargoyles, well seen from the lane itself.

★ **Nuffield** *(1937: William Morris, Lord Nuffield)* New Road — The college is for graduates and those doing research in the fields of politics, economics and the social sciences, and has established a world-wide reputation for the excellence of its academic record. The tower (the library of the college), with its distinctive stark square shape and green copper-sheathed spire, is a striking modern addition to the traditional Oxford skyline, and has already become as much a part of the view as its medieval companions. Below, the cross-shaped quadrangle with its long pool, attractively planted and stocked with fish, and the ornamental fountain, is designed in a Cotswold manor-house style, and contrasts totally with the modernity above.

★ **Oriel** *(1324: Adam de Brome; refounded 1326 by King Edward II)* Oriel Square — The Front Quadrangle was rebuilt in an old-fashioned Gothic style in 1620–4, and the chapel and hall in 1642. The chapel furnishings are almost entirely 17th century. St. Mary's Quadrangle incorporates the remains of the former St. Mary's Hall, one of the constituents of Oriel. The college takes its name from *La Oriole*, a medieval house acquired by Oriel in the 14th century. Others, though, say that it is from the architectural feature known as an "Oriel Window", one which projects beyond the line of a building and overhangs the street or garden below.

1.   Balliol College   2.   Trinity College   3.   St. Edmund Hall
4.   St. John's College   5.   Magdalen College cloisters   6.   Merton College

1

2

3

4

5

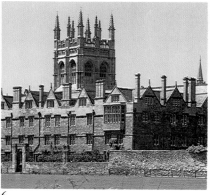

6

★ **Pembroke** *(1624: under the auspices of King James I)* Pembroke Street —
The college incorporates what is left of the almshouses built on the site in 1525 by
Cardinal Wolsey, and also includes a long stretch of the old city wall. The hall, built
in 1847–8, is one of the largest of any college, and was the last to follow the
traditional medieval design.

★ **The Queen's** *(1340: under the patronage of Queen Philippa, wife of
Edward III)* High Street — The college was entirely rebuilt in the 17th and 18th
centuries, and has no buildings earlier than 1672. The great façade on High
Street, with its domed rotunda and false colonnade, is vital to the appearance of
the street, said to be among the best of urban design in the world. The Front
Quadrangle is an excellent example of English renaissance architecture, using
classical themes but interpreting them in a distinctively English way, here using
the traditional medieval college plan. The very beautiful library (North Quadrangle)
of 1692–5 can be seen to advantage from Queen's Lane, at the rear of the
college.

★ **St. Catherine's** *(1962: Oxford University, with grants from charitable,
industrial and private sources)* Manor Road — The first college designed and
built entirely as a single scheme, and the first to use the latest concepts of
architecture and construction; hitherto, even new buildings had tended to be
traditional in style and materials. It was designed by the Danish architect, Arne
Jacobsen, and his attention to detail was such that he even produced special
designs for the cutlery and door handles: the intention was that every aspect of
the college would be in total harmony. "Catz" lies away from the city centre, near
the winding River Cherwell, but if you would like a change from the medieval and
classical styles of the older colleges, it is an interesting and attractive place to visit.
It can be reached by the pleasant riverside walk from Magdalen College.

★ **St. Edmund Hall** *(1957: but before then a Hall, associated with Queen's
College, and the direct descendant of a school founded in 1225 by St. Edmund of
Abingdon)* Queens Lane — Its ancient origins allow this college, affectionately
called "Teddy Hall", to claim that it is the oldest of all, although it is doubtful if this
can be upheld! The Front Quadrangle is the most charming in Oxford, tiny and
irregular with no side the same as another, the whole in total contrast to the
grandeur of The Queen's College on the other side of Queen's Lane. Remarkably,
the entire right (south) side and part of the far side date from the early 20th
century, but so skilful was the design that they could have been there for
centuries. The small chapel with its great leaning columns, the well, the window
boxes and the rough tiled roofs all contribute to a delightful and memorable
scene. The college library is in the ancient former church of St. Peter-in-the-East,
the fine Norman crypt of which is open to the public.

★ **St. John's** *(1437, as St. Bernard's College, by Archbishop Chichele of
Canterbury; then refounded in 1555 by Sir Thomas White)* St. Giles — The large
Front Quadrangle is partly of the 15th century, and is the only surviving part of the
former monastic college of St. Bernard, which was suppressed in 1546 by Henry
VIII. It was later completed in the 1590s. Beyond it is the Canterbury Quadrangle,
of which the south range and library were built in 1596–1601 and the remainder in
1631–6. The later work, for Archbishop Laud of Canterbury, is the finest mid-

Part of Victorian stained glass window in Exeter College

17th-century building in the city: the superb bronze statues by Hubert Le Sueur of Charles I and Queen Henrietta Maria (1633) are a feature of the quad. The North Quadrangle, to the left of the main entrance, contains a sequence of modern buildings of the last 30 years, showing how the architectural styles of this century can be successfully adapted to fit the traditional plan of an Oxford college.

★ **Trinity** *(1286: as Durham College, by the monks of Durham Cathedral, but refounded and renamed in 1555 by Sir Thomas Pope)* Broad Street — The college is unusual in that it is set well back from the road amid gardens and lawns. On Broad Street are the charming little 17th-century cottages, the last of those which once lined most of the street. Behind them, through the great iron gates, is the Front Quadrangle with its lawns and trees. The visitor then reaches the Gate Tower of 1691, and beyond is Durham Quadrangle (1417–21), part of the buildings of the old monastic college which was dissolved during the Reformation. The chapel was added in the late 17th century, and is noted for its excellent carved woodwork. Trinity is famed for its beautiful gardens, extending to Parks Road, and considered to be among finest in Oxford.

★ **University College** *(about 1249: William of Durham)* High Street — This is the college which has the most convincing claim to be the oldest in Oxford, although the story that it was founded in the 8th century by King Alfred is, sadly, just an attractive legend. However, the date of 1249 does appear to be earlier than that of any other college. There are no original buildings, as a total rebuilding took place in the 17th century. The fine Front Quadrangle dates from 1634–77, and Radcliffe Quadrangle (1716–19) was deliberately and carefully designed to an identical style, to harmonize with the earlier work. Together they present a very long and imposing façade to High Street, and the older style contrasts well with that of Queen's College opposite, and with All Souls further over to the west. Of interest, too, are the gate tower, with its statue of Queen Anne, and the 19th-century memorial to the poet Shelley, a student of "Univ" as it is usually known. The college is equal in status to all the others, and its name does not imply that it is "The University" as it is sometimes believed.

★ **Wadham** *(1610: Nicholas and Dorothy Wadham)* Parks Road — The only one of the older colleges to have been planned and built as a single composition, all at the same time. It has remained almost untouched since its completion, and has a unity of design and appearance which is of great beauty. The perfect Front Quadrangle leads on to the more irregular Back Quadrangle, which lies behind the shops and houses of Holywell Street. The hall and chapel are outstanding examples of Jacobean work, and the main façade to Parks Road, with its foreground of lawns, ranks as one of the most beautiful in Oxford.

★ **Worcester** *(1714: Sir Thomas Cookes, on the site of a monastic foundation, Gloucester College)* Worcester Street and Beaumont Street — The buildings are mainly 18th century including the larger part of the quadrangle and the gatehouse. On the south (left) side of the quadrangle are the well-preserved 13th- and 14th-century domestic buildings of Gloucester College, a most fortunate and attractive survival. The college gardens, with their lake, great spreading trees and sweeping lawns, are perhaps the finest in Oxford (except for the Botanic Gardens) and are ideal for a pleasant and relaxing walk.

Worcester College

AN OXFORD ALBUM

Of the hundreds of boys who come up to the university each October "it is only an insignificant minority who come with the ostensible purpose of learning". This was the jaundiced view of an Oxford don, A.D. Godley, in 1894 but, after a much briefer acquaintance with the university, the American John Corbin concluded that the typical Oxonian was The Slacker who even felt it necessary to apologize for attending a lecture or a tutorial. Most slackers would have enjoyed the communal eating and drinking in hall which has been described as the great ritual of Oxford scholarship. This ritual is seen to perfection in the Boar's Head ceremony at Queen's College (1). Held every Christmas Day, the custom is said to derive from the deliverance of an Oxford student who was surprised by an angry wild boar while reading his Aristotle in Shotover Forest. With great presence of mind, the student thrust the volume into the animal's mouth and made his escape. For gourmets who wished to indulge their enthusiasm beyond the college dining-hall, there was a range of social and dining clubs which provided sumptuous fare and further employment for college servants (2).

Many undergraduates had a passion for sport and even those who did not play were keen to talk about it. College cricket teams with such names as the Trinity Triflers and the New College Rabbits provided a none too strenuous way of spending summer afternoons; in 1908, the University College B team hired the old Blenheim coach to take it to a game in Wallingford (3). Corbin's slackers had a marked aversion to the river because they had little in common with keen rowing men. Eights Week, a series of bumping races between college eights, became the sporting and social event of the Oxford year with oarsmen "superb yet debonair in blazers" and "the barges and the walks and the crowded punts ... alive with femininity". The college barges (4) lined the river Isis in Christ Church Meadow, each providing a changing-room, sitting-room and spectators' deck; they were a splendid ornament to the Oxford scene.

Commemoration Week at the end of the Trinity, or Summer, term was another important event in the Oxford calendar, a social round of parties and college balls and an opportunity for flirtation between undergraduates and their friends' sisters or cousins (5). The week culminated in the Encaenia Ceremony at the Sheldonian Theatre, when honorary degrees were conferred and the university's founders and benefactors were commemorated.

Throughout the year, the undergraduate's room (6) served as home, refuge and study. To the Freshman, it must have seemed a lonely place however much he adorned it with personal effects and framed photographs. As he got to know other members of the college, he could invite them in and ply them with breakfast, hotters - crumpets, toasted teacakes and muffins - or drinks; girls, however, would rarely have been allowed to cross the threshold without a chaperone.

1.   *College chefs prepare the Boar's Head, Queen's College, about 1900*

2.   *Dining Club at University College, about 1910*

3.   College cricketers on the coach for Wallingford, 1908

4.   University College barge and crew, Eights Week 1907

5. *Friends and relations in Commemoration Week, 1909*

6. *Undergraduate's room at University College, about 1910*

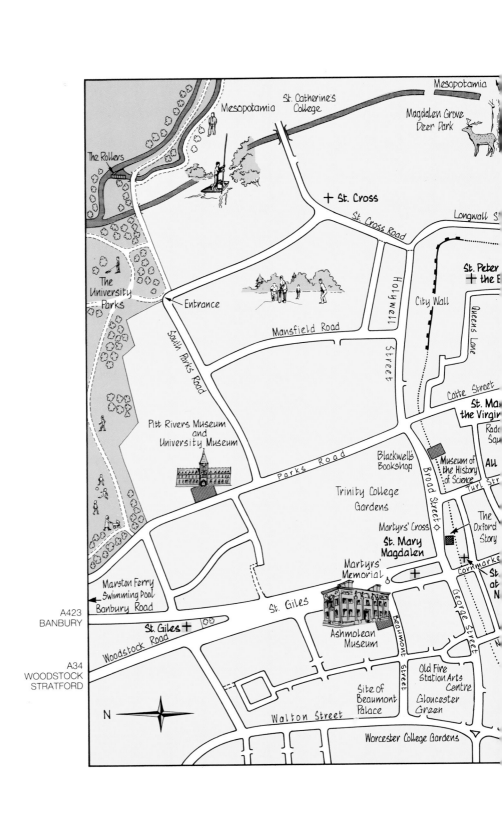

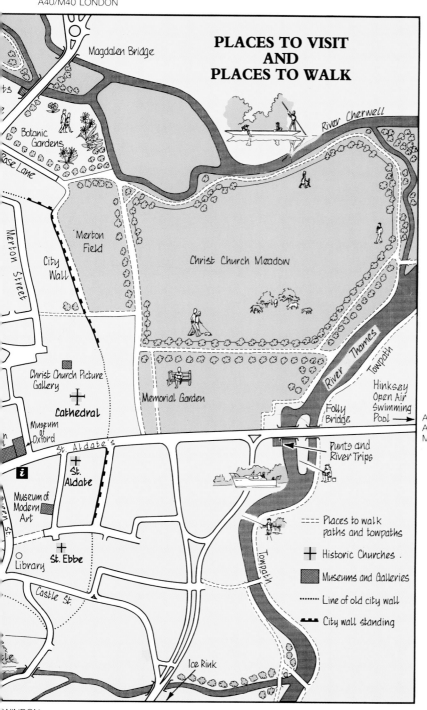

PLACES TO VISIT
AND
PLACES TO WALK

River Cherwell

Magdalen Bridge

Botanic Gardens

ase Lane

Merton Street

Merton Field

City Wall

Christ Church Meadow

River Thames

Towpath

Christ Church Picture Gallery

Cathedral

Memorial Garden

Museum of Oxford

Folly Bridge

Hinksey Open Air Swimming Pool →

A34
ABINGDON
M4

St. Aldate's

St. Aldate

Museum of Modern Art

St. Ebbe

Library

Castle St.

Punts and River Trips

Towpath

Ice Rink

Towpath

==== Places to walk paths and towpaths

✛ Historic Churches .

▨ Museums and Galleries

...... Line of old city wall

▬▬ City wall standing

Churches, Museums and Galleries

The university and college buildings are the most popular attractions of Oxford, but there is a wide range of other places of interest, including churches, museums and galleries.

Museum of Oxford (Town Hall)   The Museum of Oxford is the best way of discovering more about the city, its origins and its development. The museum, in the basement of the Town Hall (entrance in Blue Boar Street), provides a clear and informative account of how the city grew, using explanatory maps and diagrams, artists' impressions, reconstructions of entire rooms, models and displays, as well as original objects and exhibits. The museum is arranged with a section devoted to each period or theme, so that by walking around, the story of Oxford unfolds as the visitor follows the route. The permanent displays are complemented by changing exhibitions.
Open: Tues-Sat, 10am—4pm (Shop, toilets; admission free).

University Museum (Parks Road)   The building was begun in 1853 and completed in 1858, and is outstanding as an example of pleasing and functional Victorian architecture. There is extensive use of cast-iron: the museum was built only three years after the famous Crystal Palace, one of the greatest iron-and-glass buildings. The glassed roof gives plenty of light and an airy atmosphere, perfect for the display of great skeletons of dinosaurs which are one of the most impressive features of the museum. The collections are scientific, one of the aims of its founders being to provide a complement to the art treasures and collections of the Ashmolean Museum, and to serve the new scientific departments of Oxford University which were being established at this time. Of particular interest are the rocks and minerals, with splendid specimens of British geological material. The museum also has the only remains of the extinct dodo of Mauritius.
Open: Mon-Sat, 12—5pm (Shop, toilets; admission free).

Pitt Rivers Museum (Parks Road)   The museum, located behind the University Museum in Parks Road, houses collections of anthropological and ethnological material, much of it brought back by explorers and researchers in the 19th century from Africa, Asia and South America. There are many fascinating and remarkable examples of "native" art and culture: masks, weapons, pottery and utensils, costume and jewellery, as well as sculpture and carving. This is one of the finest collections in the world of this type of material.

The Pitt Rivers Museum has another building, at 60 Banbury Road, which contains collections of musical instruments and also exhibits relating to hunting and gathering societies, in the past and today. The instruments may not only be seen, but also heard!
Open: Mon-Sat, 1—4.30pm (Shop, toilets; admission free).

Cast of **Iguanodon bernissartensis,**
a vegetarian dinosaur, in the University Museum

The Ashmolean Museum (Beaumont Street) The Ashmolean, founded in 1683, is one of the world's great museums and is the oldest public museum in Britain (more than 60 years older than the British Museum). Its founder was Elias Ashmole, and he used the collection of curios brought from all over the world by the Tradescants, gardeners to King Charles I. The present magnificent buildings in Beaumont Street were opened in 1845. Of particular note are: paintings and drawings, with major collections of Michelangelo drawings, works of the Pre-Raphaelites and French Impressionists; the collection of European silver; British antiquities, including the famous Alfred Jewel; coin collections; one of the finest collections of Greek and Roman antiquities anywhere in the world, with vases, sculpture and coins; the Near Eastern and Egyptian collections; and Oriental art, including Japanese, Chinese and Indian drawing, metalwork, ceramics and textiles.
Open: Tues-Sat, 10am—4pm; Sun, 2—4pm (Shop, toilets; admission free).

Museum of Modern Art (Pembroke Street) The Museum of Modern Art, housed in a skilfully converted warehouse in Pembroke Street, close to the rear entrance to Marks and Spencer's, is a privately-owned gallery devoted to art of the 20th century. As well as permanent displays of paintings and drawings there are regular, frequently changed and very varied exhibitions and displays of modern artists' work, including paintings, printing, photography, ceramics, sculpture and textiles. Films, concerts and lectures are also regularly held. The café is excellent, as is the bookshop.
Open: Tues-Sat, 10am—6pm; Sun, 2—6pm (Shop, café, toilets; admission free).

Museum of the History of Science (Broad Street) This museum is housed in the Old Ashmolean Museum next to the Sheldonian Theatre; the building (1681) is a fine example of English Renaissance architecture. The collections are based on those of Dr. Lewis Evans, and were started in 1925. The aim is to explain and illustrate the development of scientific principles, methods and discovery of the past 400 years. The collection of early scientific instruments is probably the best and most comprehensive in the world, and there are special collections and displays of clocks and watches, astronomical and surgical instruments, and exhibits connected with electricity and photography.
Open: Mon-Fri, 10.30am—1pm and 2.30—4pm (Bookstall; admission free).

Bate Collection of Historical Instruments (Faculty of Music Building, St. Aldate's) This is the most comprehensive collection of historic European instruments in Britain, perhaps in Europe. It is particularly strong in woodwind, brass and percussion instruments, and includes many unique and remarkable examples. There are also frequent and regularly changed special exhibitions to coincide with musical events and anniversaries, or to illustrate particular themes.
Open: Mon-Fri, 2—5pm (Shop, toilets; admission free).

Christ Church Picture Gallery (Dean's Garden, Christ Church) Christ Church has the richest art collections of any college, and this purpose-built gallery displays some of its treasures. There are permanent collections of European art, including many Old Masters, and changing exhibitions of the college's very extensive collections of European drawings of the 14th — 18th centuries. There are also regular special exhibitions.

Open: Mon-Sat, 10.30am—1pm and 2—4.30pm; Sun, 2—4.30pm (Shop; small charge for admission, entrance in Oriel Square).

The Cathedral Treasury (Cathedral Chapter House, Christ Church) This is a permanent exhibition of the treasures of the cathedral and college, with fine silver and gold plate, together with changing exhibits of plate belonging to parish churches within the diocese of Oxford. It is housed in the Cathedral Chapter House, itself a superb building, which also contains a bookshop and information centre.

Open: Mon-Sat, 9am—5pm; Sun, 1—5pm (Shop, toilets; admission to the college is by the adjacent Meadow Buildings entrance, and there is a small charge).

St. Michael at the Northgate Church (Cornmarket Street) This church, the oldest building in the city of Oxford, stands where the North Gate of the city was until the late 17th century. It was built into the city wall itself, and was part of the fortifications, which helps to explain its austere appearance. It dates from the first half of the 11th century, and its small round-headed double windows are typical of late Saxon architecture. The tower is now open to the public, and from its top there is a good unusual view of the northern part of the city centre. There is also a small display of church plate and records.

Open: (Tower) Mon-Sat, 10am—5pm (in winter, until 4pm); Sun, 2—4pm. There is a small charge for admission to the Tower.

The University Church of St. Mary the Virgin (High Street) This is the parish church of the University of Oxford, the finest church in the city, and one of the most magnificent of all English town churches. Its most prominent and outstanding feature is the slender soaring spire. It was built in 1315–25. Visitors can climb to the base of the spire, and enjoy a wonderful view across the city and the surrounding hills and valleys. The interior of the church, mainly of the late 15th century, is unusually wide and light, 165 feet long, with wonderful stained glass windows and a lavish amount of decoration, monuments and memorial tablets. The unique south porch, facing on to High Street, has great twisted "barley sugar" columns, and a profusion of decoration and sculpture. The church has a very interesting brass-rubbing centre and also houses the *Oxford Experience* an audio-visual introduction to Oxford and its history. The entrance for both of these, and for ascents of the tower, is on Radcliffe Square.

Open: (Tower and Brass-Rubbing Centre) Daily, 9.15am—7pm (in winter, until 4.30pm).
(Oxford Experience) Daily, every 30 minutes from 10am—5pm.

Oxford (Christ Church) Cathedral (Christ Church, St. Aldate's)

Oxford Cathedral, the smallest cathedral in England, is the chapel of Christ Church and was, before the Dissolution of the Monasteries, the priory church of St. Frideswide. The religious use of this site dates back to the 7th century, when the original priory was founded by St. Frideswide, a Saxon princess. It was refounded as an Augustinian priory in 1122, and became very prosperous during the medieval period. In the 1520s the buildings were commandeered by Cardinal Wolsey to form the basis of his great new college, named Cardinal College in honour of its founder. Wolsey pulled down three bays of the great nave of the priory church, to make way for the quadrangle of the college, and the remainder would have been demolished also, but he fell from power and the work remained unfinished. In 1546 the priory church became the cathedral of the new diocese of Oxford, while the college was refounded as Christ Church by King Henry VIII. The college did not have a separate chapel, and so the new cathedral served a double role as it has continued to do until this date. The Dean of the Cathedral is also the dean, or principal, of the college.

Few parts of the original early medieval church are now visible, because of later alterations. The short Norman tower (early 12th century) and the stumpy spire of a century later are best seen from a distance, as the college buildings gathered around the cathedral prevent a close-up view. The spire is one of the earliest — some would say *the* earliest — in Britain, the forerunner of thousands of church spires up and down the country.

Once inside the cathedral the visitor feels a sense of height and spaciousness, even though the dimensions of the building are, by the standards of most cathedrals, small. Of particular importance is the choir, which has a superb vaulted roof of 1500, and three tiers of arches (a triforium) with carved capitals to their columns. The nave contains the remains of the shrine of the foundress, St. Frideswide. The north and south aisles and the nave have excellent and historically important Pre-Raphaelite stained glass of the 1870s, by Morris & Co. The remains of the cloister of 1499 are attached to the cathedral, and the chapter house, which contains the exhibition of cathedral treasures and the bookshop, is a good example of 13th century work.

Botanic Gardens (High Street)

The gardens are beside the River Cherwell, on the south side of Magdalen Bridge, and are approached from High Street. They are the oldest Botanic Gardens in Britain, and among the finest. Their foundation was in 1621, and was based on the collection of the naturalist and botanist John Tradescant, the gardener to King Charles I. The gardens are delightful, with an outstanding collection of rare and beautiful plants in a peaceful setting by the river. There is a walled garden with lawns and formal beds, winding woodland paths, and smooth turf sloping down to the river near the bridge (a good place to sunbathe or to watch punting). There are also large hot-houses with tropical and desert species.

Open: October-March: Mon-Sat, 8.30am—4.30pm; Sun, 10am—12pm and 2—4.30pm.
March-October: Mon-Sat, 8.30am—5.00pm; Sun, 10am—12pm and 2—6pm.
The greenhouses are open from 2—4pm every day.

Water-lilies in one of the
Botanic Gardens' hot-houses

WALKS AND OPEN SPACES

You may find that the splendours of the colleges and the magnificent buildings of central Oxford overwhelm you, or that it is a hot day and you do not want to be in crowded streets for the whole of a day. Welcome then to another Oxford! Oxford of shady walks and green spaces, of its watersides, punts and steamers. Our map shows the location of the walks mentioned in this section.

The University Parks   This popular expanse of grass, trees, walks and formal flowerbeds lies just north of the city centre, and may be entered from Parks Road beyond Keble College, or from the sharp bend where South Parks Road becomes St. Cross Road. The Parks, as they are invariably known, were laid out in the 1860s and formed part of the development of the expensive suburb of North Oxford, the tree-filled gardens and large Gothic houses of which lie along the northern edge of the Parks. This is one of the best surviving examples of Victorian park design, and its character is now carefully protected by Oxford University, which owns it. The willow-lined River Cherwell forms the eastern boundary of the Parks, and is spanned by the dramatic footbridge called Rainbow Bridge (1910). The pond at the north-east corner of the Parks is home for numerous ducks and other water birds, and a trip to feed them is a regular and popular Sunday afternoon outing. University and college sporting events are often held in the Parks, including county cricket in the summer, and there are tennis and croquet facilities.

Magdalen College Walks   These are approached through the college itself, and are a complex of paths which follow the Cherwell and its side-streams. They are charming and attractive throughout the year, at any season. In the winter, when the river is full and the leaves have fallen, they are a perfect place for a brisk walk, while in the summer they are green, cool and shady, ideal for a restful stroll well away from the noise of traffic. From the bridge at the north-west corner can be seen Magdalen College deer park, and the mill nearby is very picturesque. Birds may be seen from Magdalen College Walks, especially on snowy days in winter.

Christ Church Meadow   Christ Church Meadow (often called simply The Meadow) is the largest open space close to the centre of the city, and is a quite remarkable survival. It is only a quarter of a mile from Carfax, but is still regularly used for the grazing of cattle, as it has been for many hundreds of years. The Meadow is encircled by broad gravelled walks, laid out in the 19th century and forming an excellent circular walk along the Thames and Cherwell. It can be approached either from the St. Aldate's garden entrance to Christ Church or from Rose Lane, opposite Magdalen College. At the northern end of the Meadow is the

Cricket in the University Parks

Broad Walk, once the finest avenue of elms in Oxford, but now a shadow of its former self after the ravages of age and disease had necessitated the felling of most of the trees. It will once more be a splendid avenue, now that replanting has taken place!

The Oxford Canal   The canal was opened in the 1790s to carry coal and other commodities from the industrial areas of central England to Oxford and the Thames, and to send corn and agricultural produce in the other direction. It links the Thames with the midland canal network near Coventry. Today it is used for pleasure-craft, and is very popular for cruising and short trips, being one of the key links in the national waterways network. The tow-path may be reached from Hythe Bridge Street, which is the continuation of George Street towards the railway station. The path is a fine route for a gentle stroll and is also much used by joggers. There are brightly painted canal longboats moored at the Oxford end, and as the canal passes the edge of the 19th-century suburb of Jericho you will see the lively boat-yard, with the square tower of the church of St. Barnabas, noted for its Byzantine-inspired mosaics, beyond. Further north the canal path gives access to Port Meadow and its wide open spaces.

Punting and boating   The punt is the traditional rivercraft in Oxford (and Cambridge). It is a long, narrow and flat-bottomed boat, very low in the water, and ideal for using on the shallow marshy streams that were typical of both cities.

Punts are propelled by a long pole, which is pushed into the water until it reaches the bottom. The person punting then pushes away from the pole before quickly drawing it out again. The golden rule is not to let go of the pole!

Punts, together with more conventional rowing-boats, may be hired at three places in the city. The Cherwell Boathouse (which is also a delightful place for sitting by the river), is in Bardwell Road, off the Banbury Road about half a mile north of the Parks. The Boathouse serves teas in summer, and also has an excellent restaurant. There are places to hire punts at the western end of Magdalen Bridge (on the Cherwell), and at Folly Bridge, at the foot of St. Aldate's, on the Thames. The Thames punts have longer poles than those used on the Cherwell, because the river is deeper.

Trips by river steamer, for the few miles to Abingdon and back, or for longer distances, are available from Salters' premises in the middle of Folly Bridge. Consult Salters or the City Information Office for details of fares and timetables.

The Thames Waterside A fine view of the city, with its celebrated skyline of towers, domes and spires, may be obtained from the southern edge of the Meadow beside the Thames. The river bank here is a broad grassy stretch, very pleasant for picnicking and resting. The tow-path is a pleasant place to watch the river and its world go by — oarsmen practising, with the cox of the boat shouting instructions, or the trainer on the bank cycling along with a megaphone, river trips passing by in large steamers, and small groups of people rowing or punting in a more strenuous yet leisurely way.

Colourful punts idling on the Cherwell River

REST AND REFRESHMENT

There are many interesting and delightful places for lunch, tasty snacks and supper in Oxford. Our list of places, based on the route of the Guided Walk, though partial, will serve you well for sustenance, rest and relaxation.

The Mitre Coffee (from 11am), lunches, afternoon teas and supper; an 18th-century coaching-inn on the High Street, now altered, but once the most famous in the city — the stage-coaches left here for London.

The Turl Bar Coffee (from 11am) and lunches; part of the Mitre, it is just round the corner, tucked away on the left down Turl Street.

The Grapes Coffee (from 11am), lunches and supper; a period piece, noted for its well-preserved Victorian interior. Opposite the Apollo Theatre in George Street.

The Oxford Brewhouse Coffee (from 11am), lunches and supper; lots of atmosphere, several levels and full of nooks and crannies to sit in. In Gloucester Street, off George Street. Live jazz.

Sweeney Todds Lunches, teas and supper; a very pleasant spacious restaurant spanning three floors. In George Street near the Apollo Theatre.

The Lamb and Flag Coffee (from 11am), lunches and supper; a popular pub in St. Giles near St. John's College and with access through the quaint passage to Parks Road, Keble College and the University Museum.

Browns Coffee (from 11am), lunches, afternoon teas and supper; perhaps the most popular place to eat in the city. It is a converted garage although you would never recognize it as such, in Woodstock Road. The bread shop and patisserie, Maison Blanc, is next door, and the fashionable Little Clarendon Street is just around the corner.

The Eagle and Child Coffee (from 11am), lunches and supper; opposite the Lamb and Flag in St. Giles, it is noted for its connections with the famous Oxford author and don, J.R.R. Tolkien, who was a regular.

The White Horse Coffee (from 11am), lunches and supper; a small pub, tucked between the two Blackwell's bookshops opposite the Sheldonian Theatre in Broad Street.

The Kings Arms Coffee (from 10.30am), lunches and supper; one of the most popular pubs in the city, a favourite haunt of students and lecturers, it is situated on the corner of Holywell Street and Parks Road.

The Turf Tavern Coffee (from 11am), lunches and supper; one of the oldest buildings in the city centre and one of the cosiest public houses in Oxford, nestling under the walls of New College, and approached by the quaint narrow passageways of Bath Place and St. Helen's Passage.

The Wykeham Coffee Shop Coffee (from 10.30am), light lunches and afternoon teas; a small, cosy establishment in Holywell Street, opposite New College. Home-made cakes.

The Head of the River Coffee (from 11am), lunches, afternoon teas and supper. A successfully converted riverside warehouse, with a pleasant river terrace; situated at Folly Bridge, near to punt and boat hire stations.

The Bear Coffee (from 11am), lunches and supper; a small, cosy place noted, apart from its good food, for its remarkable collection of ties, displayed in cases around the walls. In Alfred Street, off the High.

A summer evening at the Ball

PHOTOGRAPH CREDITS

Chris Buckley: front endpaper (top), and pages 7, 11, 16, 17, 27, 29, 31, 33 (1,2,3,5), 35 and 48.
K.P. Gingell: front endpaper (middle, bottom), and pages 1, 19, 25 (top), 33 (4,6) and 55.
Rob Judges: page 25 (bottom). **Oxford City Library (Historical Collections):** pages 39, 40 and
41. **Thomas-Photos:** pages 2, 5, 9, 14, 18, 21, 22, 23, 37, 45 and 51. **Peter Upton:** front and back
covers and pages 20, 52 and 53.

SOME USEFUL TELEPHONE NUMBERS

Apollo Theatre (Box Office)	244544	Heathrow)	711312
British Rail (wait for reply		(Sundays and 6pm-7am	774611)
- calls answered in		National Express:	791579
strict rotation)	722333	Thames Transit (inc. Oxford	
British Rail 'Talking Timetable'		Tube to London)	772250
(Oxford-London)	249055	Hospital (John Radcliffe / JR II)	64711
Bus/coach information:		Information Centre	726871
Oxford South Midland -		Library (Central, Westgate)	815549
Local services	711312	Oxford Playhouse	247134
City Link (fast services:		Police Station (St. Aldate's)	249881
190 to Marble Arch and		Post Office (St. Aldate's)	814581
Victoria, London;		Tickets in Oxford	
X70 to Gatwick and		(Information Centre)	727855

Designed by Wendy Meagher
Photo-reproductions and studio work by Oxford Litho Plates Ltd., Oxford
Printed in Great Britain by KNP Group Ltd., Redditch

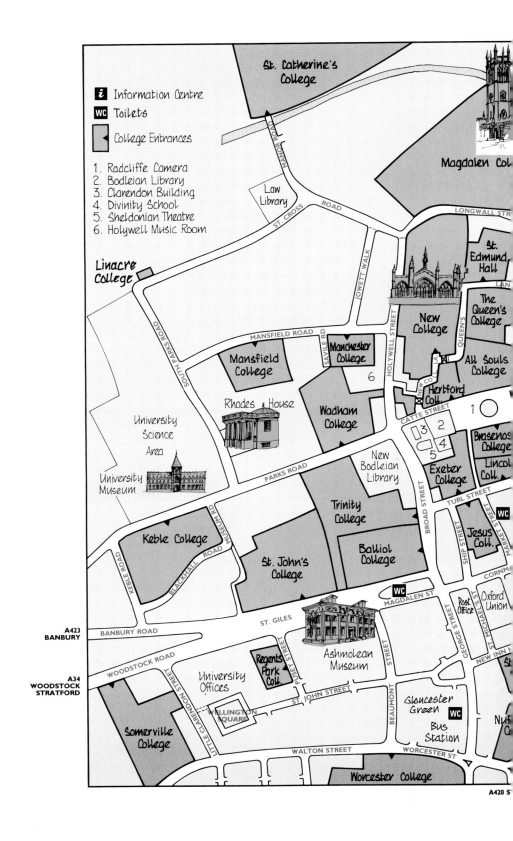

Legend

- ℹ️ Information Centre
- WC Toilets
- College Entrances

1. Radcliffe Camera
2. Bodleian Library
3. Clarendon Building
4. Divinity School
5. Sheldonian Theatre
6. Holywell Music Room

St. Catherine's College

Magdalen Col

Law Library

Linacre College

St. Edmund Hall

The Queen's College

New College

All Souls College

MANSFIELD ROAD

Mansfield College

Manchester College

Hertford Coll.

Rhodes House

Wadham College

Brasenose College

University Science Area

PARKS ROAD

New Bodleian Library

Exeter College

Lincoln Coll.

University Museum

Trinity College

Keble College

St. John's College

Balliol College

Jesus Coll.

BROAD STREET

TURL STREET

WC

A423 BANBURY

BANBURY ROAD

ST. GILES

MAGDALEN ST

WC

Post Office

Oxford Union

A34 WOODSTOCK STRATFORD

WOODSTOCK ROAD

University Offices

Regents Park Coll.

Ashmolean Museum

ST. JOHN STREET

Somerville College

WELLINGTON SQUARE

Gloucester Green

WC

Bus Station

Nuf Co

WALTON STREET

WORCESTER ST

Worcester College

LONGWALL STR

ST. CROSS ROAD

MANOR ROAD

JOWETT WALK

HOLYWELL STREET

CATTE STREET

SOUTH PARKS ROAD

SAVILE RD

KEBLE ROAD

BLACKHALL ROAD

MUSEUM RD

SHIP STREET

GEORGE STREET

BEAUMONT STREET

PUSEY STREET

LITTLE CLARENDON ST

WELLINGTON SQUARE

NEW INN

CORNM